Why Are You Wearing THAT?

A History of the Clothes We Wear

Written by Emily Hibbs

Illustrated by Ludovic Salle

Hachette UK's policy is to use papers that are natural, renewable and recyclable products and made from wood grown in well-managed forests and other controlled sources. The logging and manufacturing processes are expected to conform to the environmental regulations of the country of origin.

ISBN: 9781398325739

Text, Illustrations, design and layout © Hodder and Stoughton Ltd
First published in 2022 by Hodder & Stoughton Limited (for its
An Hachette UK Company
Carmelite House, 50 Victoria Embankment, London EC4Y 0DZ
www.risingstars-uk.com

Impression number 10 9 8 7 6 5 4 3 2 1

Year 2026 2025 2024 2023 2022

Author: Emily Hibbs
Series Editor: Tony Bradman
Commissioning Editor: Hamish Baxter
Illustrator: Ludovic Salle/Advocate Art
Educational Reviewer: Helen Marron
Design concept and layouts: Lorraine Inglis
Editor: Amy Tyrer

With thanks to the schools that took part in the development o
School, Ancaster; Downsway Primary School, Reading; Ferry L
Slough; Griffin Park Primary School, Blackburn; St Barnabas CE First & Middle School, Pershore; Tranmoor Primary School,
Doncaster; and Wilton CE Primary School, Wilton.

The publishers would like to thank the following for permission to reproduce copyright material.

Cover, p40-41, 42-43 © Berezka_Klo/Adobe Stock; Cover, p14 © Florilegius/Alamy Stock Photo; Cover, pp1, 30 © PRISMA ARCHIVO/Alamy Stock Photo; Cover, p17 © deagreez/Adobe Stock; p3, 12, 52 © Qualit Design/Adobe Stock; p4 © pololia/Adobe Stock; Tijana/Adobe Stock; p4, 29 © be free/Adobe Stock; p5, 16, 22, 41, 48 © VecTerrain/Adobe Stock; p5 © Nick Savage/Alamy Stock Photo; peter2/Adobe Stock; Rido/Adobe Stock; p6 © SofiaV/Shutterstock; Dorling Kindersley ltd/Alamy Stock Photo; p8 © Lucas/Adobe Stock; p9 © ermess/Shutterstock; mitrarudra/Adobe Stock; Taboga/Adobe Stock; p10 © fotofund/Adobe Stock; Elena Odareeva/Adobe Stock; p11 © Ursula_A_Castillo_Gomez/Shutterstock; Valentina R./Adobe Stock; Gallery Of Art/Alamy Stock Photo; coulanges/Adobe Stock; Massimo Todaro/Shutterstock; p12 © WONG SZE FEI/Adobe Stock; matiasdelcarmine/Adobe Stock; Cris Foto/Shutterstock; p13 © Lebrecht Music & Arts/Alamy Stock Photo; p14 © ACTIVE MUSEUM/ACTIVE ART/Alamy Stock Photo; p15 © moonnoon/Adobe Stock; p17 © ARCHIVIO GBB/Alamy Stock Photo; Everett Collection Inc/Alamy Stock Photo; p18 © warmworld/Adobe Stock; Olexandr/Adobe Stock; p19 © Archivist/Adobe Stock; p20 © Everett Collection/Shutterstock; Chronicle/Alamy Stock Photo; p21 © APL Archive/Alamy Stock Photo; p22 © Juan Aunion/Shutterstock; Lanmas/Alamy Stock Photo; p23 © studiostoks/Adobe Stock; Album/Alamy Stock Photo; p24 © Everett Collection/Shutterstock; p25 © xMarshall/Adobe Stock; Glasshouse Images/Alamy Stock Photo; p26-27, 28-29 © teploleta/Adobe Stock; p26 © Zzvet/Adobe Stock; p27 © Chronicle/Alamy Stock Photo; p28 © Chronicle/Alamy Stock Photo; National Museum of Denmark; gopfaster/Adobe Stock; p29 © Анастасия Боровик/Adobe Stock; p30 © Art Collection 3/Alamy Stock Photo; p31 © Lanmas /Alamy Stock Photo; Heritage Image Partnership Ltd /Alamy Stock Photo; p32 © Lebrecht Music & Arts/Alamy Stock Photo; Tony Baggett/Adobe Stock; p33 © IanDagnall Computing/Alamy Stock Photo; More/Adobe Stock; p34 © Archivist/Adobe Stock; Chronicle/Alamy Stock Photo; p35 © Granger Historical Picture Archive /Alamy Stock Photo; Directphoto Collection/Alamy Stock Photo; snaptitude/Adobe Stock; p36 © robu_s/Adobe Stock; p37 © lynea/Adobe Stock; Alexandra_K/Adobe Stock; Frazer Harrison/Staff/Gettyimages; p38 © commonthings/Adobe Stock; Anatoly Vartanov/Adobe Stock; p39 © Homer Sykes/Alamy Stock Photo; Frippitaun/Shutterstock; PA Images/Alamy Stock Photo; p40 © wectorcolor/Adobe Stock; DE ROCKER/Alamy Stock Photo; p41 © Alex Segre/Alamy Stock Photo; p42 © Heritage Image Partnership Ltd /Alamy Stock Photo; Steve Stock /Alamy Stock Photo; Kirn Vintage Stock/Alamy Stock Photo; p43 © EdNurg/Adobe Stock; p44 © BNP Design Studio/Shutterstock; p45 © Andrey Kuzmin/Adobe Stock; eurobanks/Adobe Stock; p46 © Shawshots/Alamy Stock Photo; p47 © PiercarloAbate/Shutterstock; Firma V/Adobe Stock; REUTERS/Alamy Stock Photo; p48 © sveta/Adobe Stock; lembergvector/Adobe Stock; Karina/Adobe Stock; p49 © Renaud Rebardy/Alamy Stock Photo; zakaz/Adobe Stock; p50 © Tarzhanova/Adobe Stock; p51 © Petit Pli; Yingyaipumi/Adobe Stock; p52-53 © yokunen/Adobe Stock; p52 © casejustin/Adobe Stock; Angie Makes/Adobe Stock; p53 © Happypictures/Adobe Stock; Marina Tab/Adobe Stock.

A catalogue record for this title is available from the British Library.

Printed in India.

Orders: Please contact Hachette UK Distribution, Hely Hutchinson Centre, Milton Road, Didcot, Oxfordshire, OX11 7HH.
Telephone: (44) 01235 400555. Email: primary@hachette.co.uk.

CONTENTS

WHY WE WEAR CLOTHES

What are you wearing today? Jeans and a T-shirt? A school uniform? You're probably NOT wearing a toga. Or a three-metre-wide skirt. Or shoes so pointy they need to be chained to your knees so you can walk. But if you were born at a different time or in a different place, you might be wearing just those things.

The story of the clothes you are wearing now goes back thousands of years. It goes back to a time long before catwalk shows or high-tech sports gear. Styles change, but the reasons we get dressed have stayed the same since the history of clothing began. These reasons include:

staying safe

keeping warm

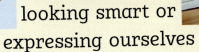

looking smart or expressing ourselves

Until 3000BCE	3000BCE–500CE	500CE–1450CE
Prehistoric times	Ancient times	Medieval times

In this book, you can discover why we wear some of the clothes we wear today. Where did we get the idea of jeans and raincoats from, and why aren't we still strutting around in pantaloons or cloaks? You will also meet some fashion icons from history and discover some funny fashions of the past.

There are so many amazing fashions from all over the world. It would fill up hundreds of books to look at them all. This book mostly focuses on fashion from European history, but there are lots of facts about clothes from other places too.

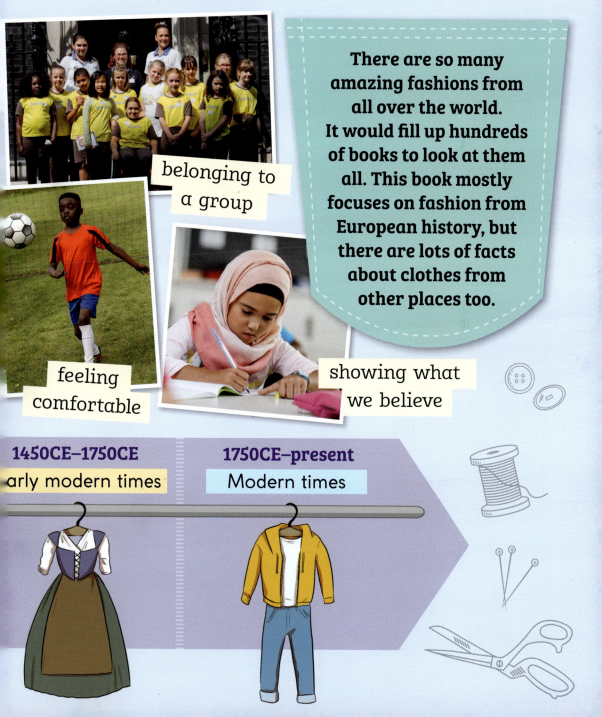

belonging to a group

feeling comfortable

showing what we believe

1450CE–1750CE
arly modern times

1750CE–present
Modern times

FIRST FASHIONS

Human beings developed over millions of years. Our early **ancestors** lived in Africa. As they set out to explore new lands, they travelled to places with colder **climates**. Historians think humans first invented clothes to keep warm in these chillier conditions.

Early clothing

At first, clothes were simple. Humans wrapped themselves in the skins and furs of the animals they killed for food. Later, we learned to cut head holes and arm holes with sharp stones and early knives. Then, we invented a form of sewing by making small slits in the furs and tying the slits together with strips of animal skin or plant **fibres**.

Animal skins rot over time, so it's tricky for historians to know exactly what these ancient clothes would have looked like or when we started wearing them.

However, historians have clever ways of putting together a picture. Here are some of the things they look for:

- 🔵 Pictures of clothes in cave paintings
- 🔵 Items used to make clothes, such as needles
- 🔵 Tiny scraps of material.

STONE AGE STYLE, 50,000 BCE

Made from the finest mammoth fur!

Sure to keep you cosy through the frostiest of ice ages!

This season's MUST-HAVE for any fashionable caveboy or girl.

Stitched together with a brand new invention: the NEEDLE!

Early sewing needle made from bird bone

Around 26,000 years ago, humans started decorating their clothes. They stitched on shells or beads made from animal bones. Wearing clothes was not just about survival anymore. People wanted their clothes to be beautiful as well as practical.

MAKING MATERIALS

About 5000 years ago, humans started to work out ways of making their own materials. One of the first materials that humans made was linen. It comes from a plant called flax. Ancient Egyptians made linen by leaving flax stems to rot in the sun. The fluffy fibres inside the stems could then be spun into clothes.

Cotton is another ancient material which we still use today. It grows in white, fluffy balls around the seeds of the cotton plant.

Secret silk

Around 4000 years ago, the Chinese started making clothes out of soft, colourful silk. There's a strange legend about how it was discovered ...

1 An empress was sitting under a mulberry tree, sipping a cup of tea ...

2 ... when something splashed into her teacup.

3 The white blob began unravelling into glossy strands.

4 Her servants worked out what it was and spun it into cloth.

The white blob was the cocoon of a type of moth caterpillar, which had fallen out of the mulberry tree. People realised the cocoon's strands could be spun into fine clothes. The caterpillars became known as silkworms and the material as silk.

Silkworms only make silk if they eat the leaves of mulberry trees.

The Silk Road

Silk was sold to the rest of the world on the Silk Road. It wasn't really one road, but many paths that went across Asia to the Mediterranean Sea. It could be very dangerous. Travellers had to deal with extreme weather as they walked across deserts and over mountains. There was also the risk of robbers.

The knowledge of how to make silk was kept secret for over 2000 years!

Cloth from animals

Wool and leather were useful materials in cold countries as they are water resistant, meaning they don't let water pass through easily. Wool is spun from fleecy animals like sheep and alpacas.

Leather is made from animal skins in a process called tanning.

In ancient times, the job of a tanner wasn't much fun. Stinky animal skins would need to be soaked, usually in old wee or dung, to clean off the blood. Tanners had to work on the edges of town as the process was so smelly.

Easy materials

Today, we often use synthetic materials – materials made in factories, rather than found in nature. In 1941, a kind of plastic material called polyester was invented. Polyester clothes didn't need to be ironed and were simple to wash.

Nowadays, clothes come in every colour of the rainbow. The dyes are usually made **artificially** in factories. In the past, most dyes were made from plants, rocks or animals.

In Mexico, the Aztecs made a bright shade of RED by crushing up tiny red beetles.

In ancient Greece, YELLOW was created using saffron, a spice that comes from crocus flowers.

Wearing BLACK was fashionable in Tudor England. Black could be made from tree bark, but the process was expensive. The clothes had to be dyed over and over again to get a strong colour.

BLUE could be created from woad or indigo plants. In the UK, police officers' uniforms were still dyed with woad until the 1930s.

In ancient Rome the most expensive colour of all was PURPLE. It was made from sea snail slime!

ALL DRESSED UP

Once humans had discovered how to make materials, cloth could be woven into different shapes. In many places, men and women wore dress-like garments for thousands of years.

Folding and draping

The Indian sari, the Greek chiton and the Roman toga are all examples of early dress-like garments. They were made from one sheet of material. It was folded or pinned in position, rather than sewn.

- The sari was invented over 2000 years before the toga. It is still worn by many Indian women.

- In ancient Greece, men wore knee-length chitons and women wore ankle-length chitons.

- To look elegant in ancient Rome, your toga needed to fall just right. You had to stay very still to keep all the folds in position.

New ideas

By the Middle Ages, explorers began to travel around the globe. As they visited new places, they discovered different materials and ways of making clothes. Up until this time, men and women had worn similar items. Most men now started wearing trouser-like hose (see page 19). Women stayed in dresses.

Fashion FACT!

Before 1330, if you wanted a tight-fitting garment, you had to be stitched into it then cut out of it! The invention of buttons meant clothes could be fastened once they were put on. Rich people's clothes had buttons at the back, so their servants could do them up. Ordinary people had buttons at the front.

In the 14th century, wealthy women wore dresses with hems that dragged on the floor behind them. Sleeves could drag on the floor too.

Underwear, outerwear

Often, outer dresses were made from materials that couldn't be washed without ruining them. Beneath their outer dresses, women wore an undergarment known as a smock which could be washed. Sometimes underskirts called petticoats were worn to make dresses stick out. From around 1600, it became fashionable for these petticoats to be visible.

Children's clothes

For much of history, children have worn the same clothes as grown-ups. Toddlers in rich families might have had to wear uncomfortable items including tight corsets, stiff ruffs and long capes. Until the 1800s, both little boys and girls wore dresses. When boys were about seven, they would stop wearing dresses and start wearing the same fashions as their fathers, including breeches (trousers). This was known as being 'breeched'.

Seriously big skirts

For a long time, wealthy women weren't expected to do much except sit around. They weren't allowed to work and had servants to help them dress. This led to some strange fashions ...

Spanish Style, 1300

Pleats held in place by pins!

Hoops made from springy whalebone!

Women in farthingales had to curtsy carefully. This was the only way they could bow to a king or queen without losing any pins!

Discover the farthingale, a new cone-shaped skirt sweeping the Spanish **royal court**!

Fashion FACT!

In the late 18th century, clothes designed for children became more common. They were looser and lighter, so children could run and play more easily. Many little girls still had to wear corsets though, so that they stood up straight.

Pretty in Paris, 1750

Who needs to sit on chairs or fit through doors? Become the talk of the town with a pannier.

Makes you wider than you are tall!

Up to two metres across to show off the details of your dress.

American Charm, 1910

Say hello to hobble skirts! Why walk easily when you can shuffle in style?

Take part in the latest craze: hobble skirt races.

Tight at the ankles so you'll only be able to totter.

Wartime wardrobes

When World War I broke out in 1914, dresses became more practical. Women were expected to help the war effort, and they could hardly do that in hobble skirts! After the war, hemlines rose up to just below the knee.

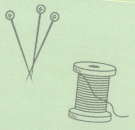

Josephine Baker (1906–1975)

When she was a young woman, Josephine moved from America to France to follow her dream of becoming a dancer. She took Paris by storm with her talent and beauty. Sometimes, she wore strange costumes made from feathers or bananas! Mostly, she wore flapper dresses, which were glitzy, fringed dresses popular in the 1920s.

In 1939, war broke out again. During World War II, many women started working in factories or on farms. They were now doing the same jobs as men. It started to become acceptable for them to wear the same kinds of clothes as men, including trousers.

Now dresses come in all kinds of styles!

TROUSERS THROUGH TIME

Today, most people think of trousers as comfortable and practical. In lots of places around the world, both men and women wear them. However, for most of history, dresses or skirts were much more popular.

Ancient trousers

The oldest pair of trousers ever found were from Central Asia. They were about 3000 years old. They belonged to a man who would have spent much of his life on horseback. Trousers are good for horse-riding, as they are flexible and there's not lots of material to get in the way. They were made from wool and fastened with string.

Togas, not trousers!

Trousers took a long time to catch on in Europe. The ancient Greeks and Romans didn't like them. They thought trousers looked silly.

Trousers didn't really become popular until about 1000 years ago. At around this time, new methods of cutting and sewing were developed, so they became easier to make. Still, some early trousers looked quite different from the styles we wear today ...

1300s: hose

Hose were tight-fitting trousers made up of two separate legs which attached to a belt or leg straps. They covered the foot, a bit like modern tights. Later, the two legs of the hose were stitched together to make one piece of clothing. Young men often wore them with a short top, so they could show off their sporty legs. As they got older, men wore longer outer robes.

Hose and doublet — not that different from modern trousers and shirt!

1500s: breeches

Breeches were trousers made from a single piece of material. They usually ended just below the knee. Men wore these with hose, stockings or boots. Sometimes, breeches would be padded to make legs look thicker!

Men wearing padded breeches

1800s: pantaloons

Breeches fell out of fashion and were replaced by pantaloons, which reached all the way down to the ankle. They looked much more like the trousers we wear today.

Men wearing pantaloons

Fashion FACT!

During the French Revolution (1789–1799), the kind of trousers you wore became a statement about which side you were on. If you were part of the rich class, you wore knee-length silk breeches. If you were part of the rebel class, you wore ankle-length trousers. Some rich people switched to longer trousers to prove they were on the side of the rebels.

Heavy-duty jeans

In 1850s USA, many people went to California to search for gold. This led to an opportunity for shop owner Levi Strauss.

1 Searching for gold was hard work. Clothes fell apart quickly.

2 Levi joined forces with a local tailor to solve this problem.

3 They created a pair of trousers made out of a tough fabric called denim.

4 They attached metal rivets to make the pockets strong enough to hold handfuls of gold!

Jeans were so hard-wearing that they became popular with many working men in America, including farmers and cowboys.

Fashion ICON

Elvis Presley (1935–1977)

When you think of Elvis, you might imagine him in a glittering jumpsuit. But when he first became famous, he had a laid-back style. He wore wide-brimmed hats and blue jeans. He looked more like a cowboy than a sparkly superstar!

THE STORY OF SHOES

Our ancestors had tougher skin on their feet, but they could still get a sore toe if they trod on a thorn! Humans invented shoes to protect their feet. In colder countries, people wore shoes made from animal skin, which went over the whole foot. People in hot countries mostly wore sandals.

Sensible sandals

Ancient Egyptians wore shoes very similar to the flip-flops we might wear to the beach. They were made from palm leaves, leather or a material similar to paper, called papyrus. People from ancient Mexico, Japan and other parts of Africa all wore shoes a bit like flip-flops too.

Free feet

Some people in the ancient world still went without shoes. Ancient Greek athletes even took part in the Olympics barefoot.

Pointy toes

In medieval times, poulaines were a popular style of shoe. The ends were stuffed with moss or horsehair. Poulaines were difficult to walk in. They sometimes had to be chained to the wearer's knees, so they didn't trip up.

People protected their shoes with wooden pattens. Pattens were like shoes for your shoes! They stopped the material getting marked by mud or soaked in puddles.

Kids kicks

Fancy footwear was for rich people only. Ordinary people had one or two pairs of sensible leather boots to last them many years. Poorer children often went barefoot, because it was too expensive to keep replacing their shoes as they grew out of them. They had to wait until their feet stopped growing to get their first pair!

High heels

When high heels were introduced in Europe during the 16th century, they were for men, not women. They were used to show status. The taller the shoe, the more important the person. Wealthy women at this time would wear platform shoes over heels.

Venice Times, 1550

CHOOSE CHOPINES!

Look down your nose at everyone you meet!

Up to 30 centimetres high!

Chopines were created by stitching silk shoes on top of wooden or cork blocks.

Fashion ICON

King Louis XIV (1638–1715)

King Louis XIV used fashion as a tool to keep his royal court in line. He came up with lots of rules for what people had to wear. His **nobles** often ran out of money trying to keep up with their king's demands. He was a short man and wore red high-heeled shoes to make himself taller. These shoes became popular across Europe.

Sports shoes

After rubber was developed in the 1850s, sporty footwear took off. The first sports shoes were known as pumps or tennis shoes. Two American companies called Keds® and Converse® were some of the first to make trainers for athletes. Their shoes are still popular today, but now people don't just wear them to do sport.

Fashion FACT!

Left and right shoes weren't invented until around 1800. Before then, both shoes were identical and were called straights.

The Converse® design hasn't changed much in 100 years.

Fashion ICON

Jesse Owens (1913—1980)

Runner Jesse Owens competed at the Berlin Olympics in 1936. He wore a pair of shoes designed by Rudolf and Adolf Dassler. The Dassler brothers would go on to found sportswear companies Puma® and Adidas®. Jesse won four gold medals in his high-tech trainers.

COAT CATWALK

Coats are complicated items of clothing. With sleeves, hoods, pockets and zips, there are lots of different parts to fit together. The first cloaks and capes were much simpler. They were made from animal fur and held together with a wooden toggle.

In ancient Greece, men and women wore a piece of cloth draped around their shoulders, known as a himation. Here's how to make your own. You will need:

⊞ bedsheet   ⊞ brooch or badge

1 Fold the sheet in half along the long edge.

2 Drape it over your right shoulder, then wrap it around your body.

3 Pin the himation in place using a brooch or badge so it doesn't slip around.

4 If it's raining, you can pull the material over your head like a hood.

Cold weather cloaks

In the Middle Ages, the most common cloak was called a mantle. Wealthy people owned different mantles for different occasions. In bad weather, they would wear a thick wool mantle, lined with fur, with a separate hood.

Fashion FACT!

In 14th century Europe, a spell of very cold weather known as the Little Ice Age meant demand for fur clothing increased. Hundreds of animals could be killed for one cloak.

Cloaks to coats

For thousands of years, everyone wore cloaks to keep warm. They were easy to make and could double as a blanket if you were travelling. However, they started to fall out of fashion in the 1800s. In 1846, the sewing machine was invented. It meant that complicated clothes could be made more quickly.

Woman wearing a fur-lined mantle

27

Long, tight-fitting wool coats, known as overcoats, became popular. Some were inspired by the style of coat worn by soldiers on the battlefield. Cloaks were still sometimes worn to fancy events, like the opera, but they were seen as old-fashioned.

The coats of today

There are many styles of coat to choose from today. Some of them have been around for a long time.

Raincoat

Some raincoats, including parkas and anoraks, are inspired by ancient **Inuit** designs. Inuit coats were originally made from sea mammal skin, and sometimes needed to be rubbed in fish oil to make sure they stayed waterproof and warm in the freezing Arctic conditions.

Modern raincoats are made from high-tech materials, such as Gore-Tex®, which **repel** water.

Trench coat

Trench coats were part of officers' uniforms during World War I. They had large pockets for tucking away maps and other useful items. After the war, trench coats became popular as everyday wear for men and women. Many of today's trench coats still have shoulder straps. Officers would have worn epaulettes on these straps, which were ornamental shoulder pieces that showed their rank.

shoulder straps

sleeve straps

deep pockets

Puffer jacket

In 1936, after a man nearly froze on a winter fishing trip, he decided to design the puffer jacket. It was stuffed with duck feathers, called down. Today, you can buy puffer jackets in lots of different colours and styles. Many are down-free, so no birds are harmed making them.

FUNNY FASHIONS

Find out about six strange or silly styles that have fallen out of fashion – for now!

Odd hose

In the Middle Ages, it was very fashionable to have half your clothes in one colour and half in another. This was known as particolour. Often, jesters took this style to the extreme with their colourful outfits.

Jesters were funny performers that entertained the rich.

Flea-furs

These days, you'd look a bit strange walking around with a dead animal draped over your arm. Fashionable people in medieval times did just that! Flea-furs were the skins of animals with the heads still attached. People hoped fleas living on their bodies might hop off onto their flea-fur instead. Sadly, it didn't work because fleas like warm living bodies.

Enormous wigs

Wigs were fashionable with wealthy people since the Middle Ages. They were a sign that you had money, as only people who didn't have to do any work could have long flowing locks. They'd get in the way if you had a job! In the 1700s, wigs took on new heights. Some were so tall that the wearers had to kneel on the floor of carriages and lean their heads out the window when they travelled.

The wigs were powdered white and scented with sweet smells. They were decorated with everything from feathers to flowers and boats to live birds!

Very rich people had their own powder room. Here, white powders and perfumes would be puffed over their wigs.

Even children wore wigs!

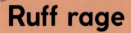
Fancy pants

Petticoat breeches were loose knee-length trousers that were in fashion around the 1660s. They were trimmed with lace, frills and metres of looped ribbons. Sometimes the legs were so wide that men accidentally put both feet through one hole.

Ruff rage

Ruffs were stiff pleated collars, popular in the 1500s. They could be made of many metres of cloth, folded up into zigzags. They could be so big that people were unable to perform everyday tasks – or even see where they were going!

Fashion FACT!

Ruffs were stiffened with starch, from flour. In the 1620s some people travelled from England to settle in America. When they got there, they struggled to find enough food to survive. They ended up boiling their ruffs and eating the starch.

Puffy padding

In Tudor times, a practice called bombasting became popular. People stuffed their clothes with horsehair or rags to make their bodies look bigger. They padded out their arms, thighs, tummies and shoulders. A square outline was very fashionable.

Fashion ICON

Queen Elizabeth I (1558–1603)

Elizabeth I was the most powerful woman in England from 1558–1603. She liked to experiment with new fashions, including puffy sleeves and big ruffs. She had a sweet tooth, and eventually her love of sugar made her teeth turn black. However, she was such a trendsetter that some people even coloured their teeth black to copy her!

Can you think of any styles around today that might look odd in a hundred years' time?

SPORTY STYLES

Up until the 1800s, there weren't really any clothes made especially for sport. Most ordinary people didn't have time for sports anyway, as their lives were taken up by work. Wealthy men might take part in outdoor activities like riding or hunting. For this, they would wear a short jacket called a riding habit.

Cricket was one of the first sports to have a uniform. Players wore all white.

By the 1850s, things had started to change. Goods were made quickly in big factories, rather than slowly in small shops. Railways were invented, so travel was faster. These changes meant people had more time to enjoy themselves.

For the first time, women started taking part in sports, such as tennis and croquet. However, they were still supposed to wear long dresses and look ladylike.

Amelia Bloomer (1818–1894)

Amelia lived in America in the 19th century. She grew tired of wearing heavy dresses that were difficult to move around in. She began wearing a knee-length skirt with baggy trousers beneath it. This became known as the bloomer costume. It didn't really catch on until bicycles became popular in the 1890s. Then, women began wearing bloomers as they were much easier to cycle in than skirts!

Modern styles

Over time, sportswear became more practical. People started wearing clothes made from comfy materials that let sweat out and air in. In the 1980s colourful outfits made from a stretchy material called Lycra® became very popular.

Modern cycling clothes are skin-tight so riders are streamlined, meaning air slips over them easily so they can go faster.

Splashy fashions

At the start of the 19th century, new railways meant people could travel to visit the seaside. Indoor pools also opened in cities. To start with, men and women visited these places to bathe, rather than swim. They wore linen undergarments and caps, and bathed in separate areas.

But people soon started swimming for exercise. Women swam in knee-length dresses, tights and shoes. Sometimes weights were sewn into their skirts to stop them floating up in the water. Men had a bit more freedom, but up until 1940 they had to wear a skirt over their swimming trunks, or wear knee-length swimsuits. Swimsuits shorter than knee-length were illegal!

Beachgoer Magazine, 1935

Brand-new bathing suit for men and boys.

Reaches the knee (so doesn't break the law)!

Swimming in style

Women's all-in-one bathing suits were invented in the early 20th century. They were considered so shocking that the first woman to wear one was arrested. Bikinis were also illegal. Though these styles are now popular with many girls and women around the globe, some choose to dress more modestly when swimming.

Fashion ICON

Halima Aden (1997–present)

Halima was born in a refugee camp in Kenya and moved to America when she was seven. When she was a teenager, she decided to become a model. In 2019, Halima became the first person to appear on the cover of *Sports Illustrated* magazine wearing an item of modest swimwear called a burkini. She is helping to make the fashion world more **inclusive** by being true to herself.

A HISTORY OF HATS

Hats are worn for all sorts of reasons, from keeping dry to staying warm. Sometimes, they're just for show!

Hard headgear

Helmets are special types of hats that protect the head from harm, whether in battle or on a bike. The first helmets were made from hardened leather. Later, helmets were made from bronze. Though their main purpose was protection, they were sometimes decorated with feathers or animal horns to impress (and scare!) the enemy.

High headdresses

Medieval women wore huge hats in a range of strange shapes. The towering steeple hennin headdress was inspired by a church spire. The heart-shaped escoffion headdress could have horns up to one metre long! Some doorways had to be made taller or wider so women could walk into a room without knocking their hats off.

Status symbols

Leaders often wear hats to show their importance. In ancient Egypt, pharaohs wore elaborate headdresses to show how powerful they were. Today, certain roles or positions still use hats or wigs as a sign of power. Some of these styles haven't changed for centuries.

Fashion FACT!

Top hats were tall black hats worn by wealthy men in the 19th century. Top hats that could squash down were worn to the opera, so they didn't block the view of the person behind.

Lawyers and judges wear old-fashioned wigs in court. These kinds of wigs were popular in the 18th century.

The style of the Pope's hat, called a mitre, is over 1000 years old!

Many kings and queens around the world still wear crowns made from gold and jewels on special occasions.

HUMANS IN UNIFORM

Today, uniforms are everywhere. You might even wear a uniform to school. Uniforms can tell us what someone's job is, or what community they are part of. It might not surprise you to discover that the first 'uniforms' appeared on the battlefield, where recognising people is really important ...

The first logos

For much of history, soldiers paid for their own armour. It was very expensive, so only wealthy people had a full suit, and it was handed down from father to son. The problem was, with everyone wearing different things on the battlefield, it was easy to mistake your friend for your enemy. Knights started marking their armour with crests and emblems to show who they were fighting for. These became coats of arms.

Knights wearing armour showing coats of arms

Team colours

The history of football kits isn't so different from the history of armour! Players used to provide their own kit, so everyone wore different shirts, trousers and leather boots. This made it tricky to tell teammates from opponents on the pitch. Teams started wearing sashes or caps in the same colours.

By 1870, many teams were wearing full uniforms. At this time, most football clubs were from private schools, so their team colours were taken from their school uniforms.

By the 1900s, football had become a sport for working class people, too. Teams had to write their colours on a list, so there weren't any clashes at matches.

Fans show their support by wearing their team's football kit. The first team to make kits for fans was Leeds United in the 1970s.

School uniforms

One of the first schools to have a uniform was Christ's Hospital in the 1500s. It was a charity school for poor children, which provided them with a blue cloak and yellow stockings. Other schools soon introduced uniforms too. It was a good way of teaching students to dress smartly and making them feel part of a group.

Christ's Hospital students still wear the traditional uniform today.

Boys who go to Harrow School still wear straw hats and tailcoats. They don't have to wear their hats on windy days though.

Uniforms for jobs became common in the 1800s. Rail workers wore blue jackets and flat-peaked caps. Bakers and milkmen wore white clothes and white caps.

Specialist suits

Certain jobs need specialist uniforms, such as scrubs for doctors and camouflage for soldiers. Some careers require very special uniforms.

To survive in Space, astronauts need a suit that protects their body from extreme heat and cold.

SPACE-AGE SUIT

Comes with built-in water and oxygen.

Takes just 45 minutes to put on!

With free cooling underwear.

Divers also need special equipment. Early diving suits were made of waterproof leather, with heavy helmets and weighted boots.

This kind of diving suit was used for over 100 years.

Modern SCUBA equipment means divers can stay underwater for longer. It contains air, delivered into the diver's mouth through a tube.

FASHION POLICE

It's no fun being told what you can and can't wear. In the past, rulers often came up with dress codes to keep control of their people.

ANCIENT ROME

Only citizens can wear togas. Slaves and visitors are not allowed.

MIDDLE AGES

Hear ye, hear ye! Englishmen in Ireland may not have Irish hairstyles.

TUDOR ENGLAND

Ordinary people are not allowed to wear fine materials, including silk, satin or velvet. They must only wear wool from English sheep, to protect the English wool trade.

Queen Elizabeth I said these laws were to stop young men becoming bankrupt. It is more likely that she wanted to make sure the middle classes didn't dress in finer clothes than the upper classes.

17th CENTURY RUSSIA

BY DECREE OF **TSAR** PETER THE GREAT: all nobles must get rid of their old-fashioned fur jackets and robes, and start wearing trousers. They must also cut off their beards.

19th CENTURY FRANCE

PUBLIC NOTICE: Women are now allowed to wear trousers but ONLY if they have written permission from the police.

This law wasn't officially changed until 2013!

Though some of these laws might seem funny, people who broke them could be fined. Or they could end up in the **stocks**, having rotten food thrown at them! People have even died for what they've worn. Joan of Arc, a medieval French heroine, was executed in 1431. Among other reasons, people weren't happy that she wore hose, rather than dresses.

Designed to divide

Throughout history, laws have sometimes forced people to wear something that shows what religion or group of people they belong to. Around 1000 years ago, Jews and Muslims living in Egypt had to wear bells on their clothes. Less than a 100 years ago, Jews in Germany had to wear a yellow star. This is a form of **discrimination**.

Who can wear what?

Most countries don't have laws about what people can and can't wear anymore. However, some people still think that certain clothes or colours are for boys only, and some are for girls only. As you have found out in this book, the rules about who can wear what are always changing. Shouldn't everyone be able to wear what they want?

In lots of **cultures** boys wear dress- or skirt-like items, such as the gho in Bhutan or the kilt in Scotland. These aren't the same as dresses or skirts, but there's no reason boys can't wear them either!

Fashion ICON

Harry Styles (1994–present)

Harry grew up in the UK and always dreamed of being a singer. He shot to fame with boyband One Direction, before going solo. He enjoys experimenting with fashion and believes people should be free to wear whatever they like. He appeared on the cover of *Vogue* magazine wearing a beautiful frilled gown.

THE FUTURE OF FASHION

Fashions used to change slowly. People had a few items of clothing that they wore over and over again, until they fell apart. Then they might patch them up and carry on wearing them. Today, big factories can make lots of clothes quickly. This means clothes have become cheaper to buy. Lots of us now buy new clothes long before our old ones have fallen apart. But what's the real cost?

What is fast fashion?

Fast fashion is a term used to describe cheap clothing that is made very quickly. Factories churn out lots of clothes to fit in with new trends. Sometimes the clothes are not very well made. People buy lots of fast fashion items, and often throw them away after a couple of wears.

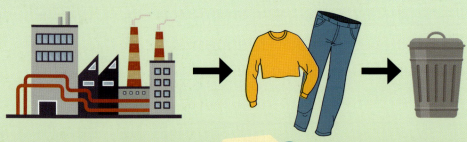

Here are a few problems fast fashion causes:

- ⊞ Fast fashion factories pump out harmful gases that cause global warming.
- ⊞ Waste from factories contains chemicals, which end up in the sea and harm sea life.
- ⊞ Fast fashion is usually made from fabrics which contain plastic. Plastic takes a long time to break down and might not disappear for hundreds of years.
- ⊞ Fast fashion is cheap to buy, which means it has to be cheap to make. Often companies making fast fashion don't pay their workers very much. They have to work long days in bad conditions and sometimes can't afford food or shelter.

Workers of fast fashion companies in Bangladesh demonstrate for better working conditions.

Fashion FACT!

The average person gets through about 310 pairs of shoes as they stomp through life. Around 300 million pairs of shoes end up in landfill each year.

Fashion forward

In the future, we need to make sure the fashion industry doesn't harm the planet or hurt workers. We all have a part to play. Here are a few things you could do:

- Buy clothes when you need them, rather than want them.
- Buy your clothes second-hand from charity shops.
- Check up on what clothing companies are doing to protect their workers.
- Buy clothes made from eco materials that don't contain plastic.

Clothes can be made out of all kinds of eco materials, including hemp, bamboo and even banana!

Futuristic fashions

As well as going greener, the fashion industry might also go smarter. High-tech clothes are already hitting the shelves and this trend looks set to continue.

Power dressing

Scientists are developing clothes with tiny electric wires hidden in the stitching. Your T-shirt could harness your body heat while you go about your day. It could turn the heat into electricity to charge your phone!

Growing clothes

A designer named Ryan Yasin has created clothes for children that grow with the wearer. Inspired by the art of paper folding, known as origami, these clothes get longer and wider as children grow.

Dressing digital

In the future, we might even wear digital clothes and 'download' our new looks. By wearing special glasses that alter reality, we'd be able to see each other's new styles instead of the old clothes we're actually wearing. We could try dresses that shimmer in every colour of the rainbow or trousers that change pattern as we walk!

WHO'S YOUR FASHION ICON?

Discover your historical fashion icon with this quiz!

★ ★ ★ ★ ★ ★

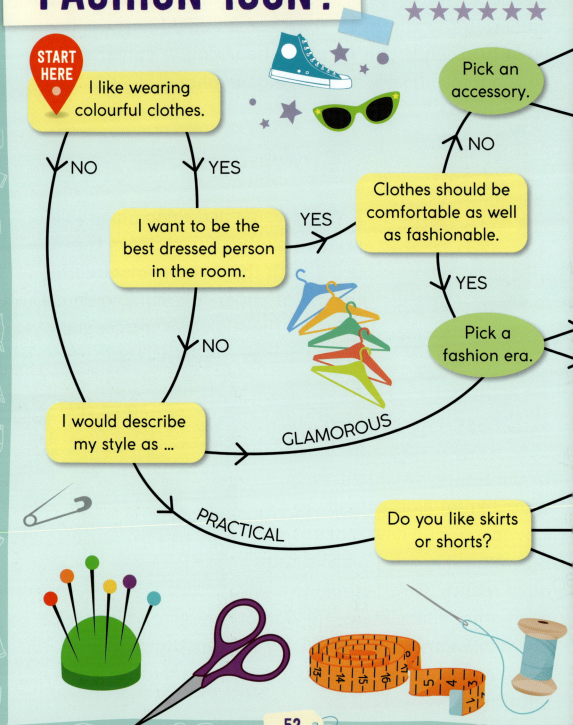

START HERE

I like wearing colourful clothes.

NO

YES

I want to be the best dressed person in the room.

YES

NO

I would describe my style as ...

GLAMOROUS

PRACTICAL

Pick an accessory.

NO

Clothes should be comfortable as well as fashionable.

YES

Pick a fashion era.

Do you like skirts or shorts?

King Louis XIV

You are a trendsetter who likes trying out new looks. You don't mind if your friends copy your style. It just proves they think you have great taste!
Signature colour: red

Queen Elizabeth I

You like wearing fabulous, colourful clothes. Some people might think a few things in your wardrobe are a bit strange, but you're happy to stand out from the crowd.
Signature colour: gold

Harry Styles

You love showing your personality and mood through how you dress. You're at your happiest when experimenting with new styles and looks.
Signature colour: purple

Josephine Baker

You like to wear glitzy outfits every now and then. But it's important to be able to run, dance and move in your clothes too. You think fashion should be fun!
Signature colour: silver

Jesse Owens

You're an active person who likes to wear sporty clothes. Perhaps you own a pair of cool trainers?
Signature colour: blue

Amelia Bloomer

Practical clothes are for you. You're not too fussed about following the latest trends and would rather be comfy.
Signature colour: black

MODERN DAY

1920s

SKIRTS

SHORTS

BOTH

GLOSSARY

Ancestor – A relative from a long time ago.

Artificial – Made by human beings, rather than found in the natural world.

Climate – The weather conditions of a place.

Culture – The way of life of a group of people.

Discrimination – The unjust treatment of groups of people, sometimes based on their race or religion.

Evolved – Developed over time.

Fibre – A thread.

Inclusive – Not leaving anyone out.

Inuit – A group of people native to parts of Greenland, Alaska or Canada.

Noble – A person of high rank.

Repel – To not allow something through, such as water.

Royal court – The nobles who live in a king or queen's home, or go there often.

Stocks – A wooden frame with holes for a criminal's hands or feet.

Tsar – A king of Russia before 1917.

INDEX

CHAT ABOUT THE BOOK

1 Read page 10. What does a 'tanner' do?

2 Queen Elizabeth I has been described as a 'trendsetter'. What is a 'trendsetter'?

3 Why was purple dye so expensive in ancient Rome?

4 Go to the chapter, 'Trousers Through Time'. What was the main difference between breeches and pantaloons?

5 How do the illustrations on page 26 help the reader?

6 Go to page 50. Read 'Fashion forward'. What is the main point the author is trying to make?

7 Why do you think the author included the chapter, 'Funny Fashions'?

8 If you travelled back in time, which item of clothing would you least like to wear?